Stanford Patriarchs

Also from Westphalia Press
westphaliapress.org

Stanford Patriarchs

Preliminary Notes on the Prosopographical
Significance of the Beards, Dundrearies, and
Muttonchops of the First (Rather Anonymous)
Trustees of Stanford University,
with the Rare Bancroft Company Edition of the
Founding Documents

Introduced by Paul Rich

WESTPHALIA PRESS
An Imprint of Policy Studies Organization

Westphalia Press
An imprint of Policy Studies Organization
1527 New Hampshire Ave., NW
Washington, D.C. 20036
info@ipsonet.org

ISBN-13: 978-1-63391-362-2
ISBN-10: 1-63391-362-7

Cover design by Jeffrey Barnes:
jbarnesbook.design

Daniel Gutierrez-Sandoval, Executive Director
PSO and Westphalia Press

Updated material and comments on this edition
can be found at the Westphalia Press website:
www.westphaliapress.org

THE DOORS THROWN OPEN

Senator Stanford — "It is all for you, my boy, and for the coming generations. My ambition is now satisfied. I have less desire to be President than to be founder of an institution that will make Presidents!"

Dr. Paul Rich is a graduate of Harvard and of The University of Western Australia. For nearly ten years he was a government adviser in the Arabian Gulf shaikhdom of Qatar. Among those books he has written or edited are several regarding the influence of the rituals of education, including *Elixir of Empire*, *Chains of Empire*, and *The Invasions of the Gulf*. Hoover Institution Fellow at Stanford, he is a Fellow of the Royal Historical and Royal Numismatic Societies, and of the Royal Anthropological Institute and College of Preceptors.

Dedicated to the scholars of the Hoover Institution, and especially to the admirably bearded Richard Sousa.

The first president of Stanford, David Starr Jordan, addresses the university's opening ceremonies on October 1, 1891. Senator and Mrs. Leland Stanford are seated at left.

STANFORD BEARDS AND MUTTONCHOPS

Video barbam et pallium: philosophum nondum video. (I see the beard and
the cloak: I have yet to see the philosopher.) — Tertullian

Prosopography is collective biography. It is generally most effective
when the group studied is a small and cohesive one. Investigating the
commonalities of a large group such as the inhabitants of the Manhattan
telephone directory might yield interesting statistics. But the exercise
would not be true prosopography as historians commonly think of
prosopography.

Those Founding Fathers of the Republic who assembled at
Philadelphia, the seasick passengers of the Mayflower, or the worthy original
trustees of the Leland Stanford Junior University, are another matter. These
are groups limited enough and well-documented enough in their origins and
their destinies to attract the prosopographer. Mining the archives and
studying the collective significance of their ethnic backgrounds, occupations
of their parents, educations, vocations and avocations can produce interesting
results. Indeed, taking the process a step further, a continuing prosopography
of the ongoing roll of Stanford trustees has potentially more to offer in some
respects than a study of the patriots or passengers. The Stanford list has been
immersed and perpetuated in the legal equivalent of the waters of youth,
corporate eternity. Thus the evolution of American society through the years
and its effects on Stanford's board can be charted. The changes in the
composition of the board mirror the eventual and proper, if sadly tardy,
enfranchisement of African-Americans, Asian-Americans, Women-
Americans.

An interest in the founding trustees which became a pursuit was
piqued by a reference in the scarce Bancroft Company pamphlet of 1888
reproduced in this little monograph. One of the original trustees, N.W.
Spaulding, is introduced as Grand Treasurer of the Grand Lodge of Free
and Accepted Masons of California.

Senator Stanford had been a man of sometimes curious and
unconventional beliefs. His appointment of Spaulding was a reminder of the
fact that Stanford himself had been thought to be an active Freemason. Had
many of the original group been Freemasons? Here was a fine
prosopographical challenge: to see if there was just a whiff of cabalism in the
founding, albeit of a respectable sort.

Research shows Stanford was and many of his friends were members of the Masonic fraternity. Dr. Norman Tutorow touches on this in a most useful paper written for the DeWitt Historical Society (*The Early Years of Leland Stanford*, Ithaca, New York, 1969), and in his subsequent study *Leland Stanford: Man of Many Careers* (Pacific Coast Publishers, Menlo Park, 1971). Stanford applied to a subordinate or "blue" Masonic lodge in Port Washington, near Milwaukee, in 1849. He took the Entered Apprentice and Fellowcraft degrees and then became a third degree or Master Mason in 1850. Subsequently he was a founding member of another blue lodge at Cedarburg, Wisconsin; when he came to California, he joined a lodge in Michigan City. The significance to the Masonic affiliations of the early trustees is discussed in another of the essays that comprise *Stanford Icons*, this modest trilogy about Stanford's rituals and search for symbols.

The first Stanford trustees well may be admirable subjects for a prosopography that eventually unearths much antiquarian wisdom. However, because of the circumstances surrounding the establishment of the university they from the beginning lacked any chance of achieving the eminence of the Signers at Philadelphia or the deification of those somewhat pious ancestors who landed at Plymouth Rock. Stanford University was the inspiration of Mr. and Mrs. Stanford, and there was no ambiguity about who were the patresfamilias. Perhaps it is rather more in order to praise the trustees for their ability to stand quietly aside and not meddle while the Stanfords poured out their gifts.

Orrin Lesley Elliott, who was Registrar of the University from 1891 to 1925, remarked in his exemplary book *Stanford University: The First Twenty-Five Years* (Stanford University Press, 1937) that until Mrs. Stanford finally agreed to surrender the absolute authority held by her under the Founding Grant, that the board was a "shadowy body without powers or duties". Such seems a fair estimate. When she did turn over control in 1903, only five of the gentlemen whose weighty visages peer from these pages remained alive: Horace Davis, George E. Gray, Timothy Hopkins, Thomas B. McFarland, and William M. Stewart.

The educational views of this portentous group thus are of secondary importance. They must take a definite backseat to the attitudes and courage of Mrs.Stanford, who after her husband's death in 1893 persisted with the vision of a great university and never lacked ideas. The Bancroft booklet then is misleading, albeit probably (but not certainly)

Wedding picture of the Stanfords, 1850

Mrs. Jane Stanford

unintentionally. In all honesty the trustees' portraits that figure so prominently could have been omitted if educational influence was the criteria; one alone of Mrs. Stanford would have sufficed.

While accepting this caveat, there are other reasons that the pictures of the trustees do have lasting interest and deserve resurrection. Perhaps no other American university of Stanford's rank is as fortunate in having such a fine group of portraits of its original (albeit quiescent) rulers. The age of comparable universities has something to do with this. Harvardians would give much to possess a set of engravings of their founders. A portrait of John Harvard has not survived, let alone those of members of the Massachusetts legislature that technically were the founders in 1636. (John died two years after the university was established, and it was his bequest of books that won him a bargain-priced immortality.)

The neglected Bancroft document potentially makes a contribution on several levels of social history. Therein lies a tale from another university, sometimes known as the Stanford of the East Coast. Profesor Frederick Merk was teaching a survey course. In one lecture he asked for reflection as he read a letter from Lafayette to Washington. The stuff of historical scholarship! Students listened intently at a description of how the war was going, scribbling down ideas but ignoring pleasantries about taking tea in saucers at someone's house. Hands were eagerly raised when Professor Merk asked for the import.

Those offering military and political speculations were disappointed. The letter, Professor Merk warned, could not be taken as conclusive evidence about the events of the time because the writer and recipient had several axes to grind, for themselves and for posterity. Real understanding of the events would come only from examining a variety of sources. *But, the letter could stand as conclusive evidence that well-bred people poured tea from the cup into the saucer to cool the liquid.*

The values of the Bancroft Company's nonpareil are similar to those of Lafayette's letter. Unsupported, it offers those who are uninitiated into Stanford University's history only a limited and possibly incorrect impression about the early days of "The Farm". Taken alone, the impressive engravings of the trustees in the booklet might create an inaccurate impression regarding the power structure in the founding period. As everyone with the slightest acquaintance with the university's history knows, that byzantine topic must be considered primarily through the lives of the Senator and Mrs. Stanford, and only after that by exploring the motives of eminences such as David Starr Jordan and the early professoriate.

Yet as remarked above, the likenesses of the trustees depicted in the Bancroft inauguration brochure make contributions to history in other ways. For example, they are an excellent indication of how the members of the California Establishment of the period were dressed and barbered, or at least of how they wished to be represented as looking. *The apparel oft proclaims the man. – Hamlet, i.3.*

Before picking upon any of the individual distinctions in trustees' appearance, the reader may be struck by a collective sober uniformity. From the perspective of more than a hundred years, these stalwarts can look like a convention of undertakers. The members of no present governing board, not excepting those of the most conservative institution, could show such extreme unanimity of dress. Even the buttons seem conformist, flat and ordinary; there is not a single button displayed by any of the gentlemen that is ornamented.

In *The Psychology of Clothes* (Hogarth Press, 1930), J.C.Flügel wrote about "The Great Masculine Renunciation" and how the man of the period had given up a right to ornamentation: "So far as clothes remained of importance to him, his utmost endeavours could lie only in the direction of being 'correctly' attired, not of being elegantly or elaborately attired." Flügel believed (unsurprisingly) that the display of a uniformity of dress was an expression of duty and self-control. What he would make of current Stanford taste in personal toilet is problematical.

He contended that the evolution of clothes produced useful scholarly insights. How vestigial a utilitarian feature became was noteworthy. One example is his attention to the *nicks* or *cut-outs* of men's coats, the points dividing collars from lapels. Nicks in the coats of most Stanford trustees were ornamental. (Nicks in the coats worn by Gray and Crocker, and possibly others according to one's interpretation, remained utilitarian.) Flügel comments, "The clothes we wear, especially the clothes of men, have many vestigial features, features that have no utility at present, but which can be shown to have been useful in the past."

The book's portraits are arranged in the order in which Mr. and Mrs. Stanford named the trustees in presenting the grant of gift on November 11th 1885. All twenty-four of the trustees were present except Shafter, Deady, Miller and Field. (Horace Davis did later maintain that only Field and Deady were absent, which evidently misled Orrin Elliott in his history.) The deed of gift was an elaborately decorated parchment "in the old illustrated style". It was an auspicious moment. At the Centennial of Stanford's founding in 1985, Professor Don Fehrenbacher gave an address in which he set the event in perspective: "By 1885, construction of the transcontinental railroads was largely finished, the great buffalo herds of the Plains had been exterminated, and the Indian wars were virtually over...Horatio Alger had written most of his popular books (including the *Ragged Dick, Tattered Tom* and *Pluck and Luck* series) and Russell Conwell in his lecture *Acres of Diamonds*, which he would deliver more than 6,000 times before he died, was telling Americans: 'You ought to be rich; you have no right to be poor.'"

Besides Leland Stanford, the following are the subjects of the plates, noted with some comments about their appearance. Only two are clean shaven.

William Ashburner   *clean shaven waistcoated*
Isaac Sawyer Belcher   *bearded waistcoated*
John Boggs *bearded stickpin*
John Q. Brown   *bearded waistcoated*
Charles F. Crocker   *moustached stickpin*
Horace Davis   *bearded*
Matthew P. Deady   *bearded*
Henry Lee Dodge   *bearded waistcoated*
Stephen J. Field   *bearded waistcoated glasses bald*
George Edward Gray   *muttonchopped waistcoated*
Charles Goodall   *bearded waistcoated*
Creed Haymond   *bearded*
H.W.Harkness   *moustached waistcoated*
Timothy Hopkins   *moustached*
T.B. McFarland   *bearded waistcoated*
John F. Miller   *moustached stickpin*
Lorenzo Sawyer   *bearded waistcoated*
Irving M. Scott   *moustached waistcoated*
James McMillan Shafter   *bearded waistcoated*

Nathan W. Spaulding   *bearded waistcoated*
Francis E. Spencer   *muttonchopped stickpin*
Josiah Stanford   *muttonchopped waistcoated*
Wm. M. Stewart   *bearded waistcoated*
Alfred L. Tubbs   *bearded*
Henry Vrooman   *clean shaven waistcoated*

The trustees are a hairy lot. As late as the 1860s beards were regarded with suspicion, and wills were probated in which heirs were cut off if they grew facial hair. This situation had changed markedly in the ensuing two decades, but the 1880s nevertheless were a transitional period in men's hair styles. Beards were increasingly associated with the middle aged and elderly. Clean-shaven faces, rare in the 1870s, were more frequent. (Penelope Byrde in *The Male Image* is somewhat dogmatic when she states, "The hair was generally shorter by the 1890's and virtually every respectable middle-class man wore a beard which was regarded as the outward, visible sign of the philistine by aesthetes of the 1880's and 1890's, who were deliberately clean-shaven and very often wore their hair longer than was the respectable fashion. Beardless men were thought to look more sensitive and 'artistic' until the end of the century.") Side-whiskers were gradually going out of fashion and large droopy moustaches were on the increase. Hair was no longer brushed over the ears as much as it once was, and was often brushed straight back rather than side parted. The portraits indicate that was welcomed.

Possibly then a careful look at the portraits raises questions about just how conformist a group and how fixed a society is involved. Richard Corson remarks in *Fashions in Hair: The First Five Thousand Years* that the times were changing ones in which "The question was no longer whether or not to wear whiskers but simply what kind. Side-whiskers, beards and moustaches were all being worn in any combination and in whatever shape happened to suit the individual fancy." The "timid sproutings" of earlier decades had become wondrously pendant side-whiskers called dundrearies (George Gray, Francis Spencer) and muttonchops (Josiah Stanford), as well as moustaches such as the soup strainer or walrus (John Miller) — and expressive beards like the billie (John Boggs).

Neckwear and collars of Stanford's trustees similarly reflect a transitional era. Collars could be stiff and upstanding or turned down, and ties could be held in place with a pin or tied in a bow. The most varied item in the dress of the trustees is the collar; there are almost as many styles represented as there are trustees. The very high ones were fashionable, although wearers complained of sore necks.

The portraits suggest that most of the trustees either tied their own ties or bought very clever ready-to-wear ones. (Admittedly suspicions are aroused by a tie such as worn by Alfred Tubbs, with its extremely narrow band.) Those like Wm. Steward and Creed Haymond, whose beards effectively concealed all, will remain for the moment an enigma. Doriece College, whose book *Collars, Stocks and Cravats* is authoritative, claims that in fact most men tied their own ties: "A large number of 19th Century cravats with bows, whether sheer or three layers of fabric, suggest by their curves and free arrangement that they were tied when donned. American portraits show that free-handed bows predominated over permanent ones throughout nine decades of the 19th century...". Sarah Levitt in *Victorians Unbuttoned* is considerably less sure: "Those privileged enough to have time and perhaps a valet to tie their tie heartily despised the ready-made version. But the thousands who were not prepared to stand in front of a mirror every morning creating difficult arrangements continued to patronise them, with only a few doubts as to their respectability." In G. and W. Grossmith's novel *Diary of a Nobody* (1892), a companion's criticism of "a made-up tie that hooks on" causes the hero to reflect, "This seems rather personal, and twice I caught myself looking in the glass of the chiffonier. For I had a tie that hooked on — and why not?"

Perhaps someday the descendants of the first twenty-four will loan artifacts for an exhibit and various questions about trustee attire will be resolved. Lacking full-length views, one can only speculate about the exact nature of the coats. Some appear to be full morning coats. Those which have a long curve from the second button down so that more of the waistcoat shows were sometimes called "university" coats. The term lounge jackets or reefers was used for coats that were shorter than morning coats.

In keeping with the moral tone, there is very little jewelry in evidence. John Boggs has an attractive stickpin and the pin worn by Senator Miller just possibly is a sign of mourning, as sometimes a pin with the departed's initial was worn as a token of respect. Those who wear studs are not depicted with flashy ones.

This is not the first consideration of sartorialism and the founding of Stanford; Senator Stanford's clothes have been the source of a little controversy. A familiar story is that of the visit of the Stanfords to President Charles Eliot at Harvard, and the account of the Stanfords asking Eliot how much it would cost to build a university like Harvard. When a surprised Eliot gave a figure of five to six million, Mrs.Stanford supposedly said, "Oh, Leland, we can do it."

As Norman Tutorow points out in his biography of Leland Stanford, the story gives an impression that the Stanfords were slightly naïve about the problems in founding a major university. The culprit was Eliot's son, Revd. Samuel Eliot, who with each retelling added 'color'. Eventually he arrived at an amusing story about "a shabby little man and shabby little woman" who went calling on the great Harvard president. As Professor Tutorow emphasises, the Stanfords were not little in either their girth or their intelligence. Senator Stanford weighed more than 240 pounds when he called on Eliot. They were hardly shabby in dress. Mrs. Stanford owned more than a million dollars of jewelry. Senator Stanford was known as conservative or old-fashioned in attire, but "his suits were of the best Irish linen".

Although the announcement of the gift was greeted with approval in most quarters, there were accusations that Mr. Stanford was unhappy at not being on the University of California board, that he was trying to win political favor, or that the idea was actually a real estate promotion scheme. In respects, therefore, the Bancroft Company booklet may be regarded as the first Stanford University foray into public relations, and must have had Senator Stanford's imprimatur.

As for the authenticity of the pictures themselves, photographers and engravers of the day were just as sensitive to the customer's egos as today. The appearance of only one blatantly bald gentleman — considering the age of the trustees surely a few more would have been normal — does suggest some gentle editorial intervention.

All this is minor compared to the tremendous longterm significance of the events commemorated. The booklet despite its obscurity is undoubtedly one of the most outstanding of all early Stanford University memorabilia. It has an unappreciated importance, and its semi-official status and evident purpose as a response to contemporary press criticisms are apparent.

The story that it tells, to quote from its pages, is of a grand idea, one pursued with unique singleness of purpose. If the first trustees were largely bystanders because of the donors' extraordinary interest in the project, the fact remains that they were the first friends of Stanford University.

Just as significantly, the trustees were the guarantee that the ambitious plan would survive Mr. and Mrs. Stanford. So it did, as that remarkable couple fully anticipated. Of many institutions it is appropriate, if hackneyed, to remark that the founders could not have have dreamt of the future success. That was not the case with Leland and Jane Stanford, who were determined on greatness.

✸ ✸ ✸

The

Leland Stanford Junior University

Palo Alto, Santa Clara County, California

THE

Leland Stanford Junior

UNIVERSITY

❉

PALO ALTO, SANTA CLARA COUNTY, CALIFORNIA

❉

SAN FRANCISCO
THE BANCROFT COMPANY
1889

HON. LELAND STANFORD

THE

Leland Stanford Junior University

SENATOR STANFORD'S PLAN FOR ITS ORGANIZATION

THE GRANT FOUNDING AND ENDOWING THE UNIVERSITY

DESCRIPTION OF THE PROPERTY EMBRACED IN GRANT

PORTRAITS OF THE TRUSTEES

THE grand idea of Leland Stanford, to found and liberally endow
a great University in California, has attracted the attention and
admiration of the civilized world. Never before, in any country,
has the mind of man conceived a grander or nobler scheme of public
benefaction, and few individuals have had the power, even if they had
the will, to devote such immense wealth to the benefit of humanity.
When the intention of Senator Stanford to found a University in
memory of his lamented son was first announced, it was expected
from the broad and comprehensive views which he was known to
entertain upon the subject, that his plans, when formed, would result
in no ordinary college endowment or educational scheme ; but when
these plans were laid before the people, their magnitude was so far
beyond the most extravagant of public anticipations that all were
astonished at the magnificence of their aggregate, the wide scope of
their details, and the absolute grandeur of their munificence. The
brief history of California as an American State comprises much that
is noble and great, but nothing in that history will compare in grandeur with this act of one of her leading citizens. The records of history
may be searched in vain for a parallel to this gift of Senator Stanford

LORENZO SAWYER

to the State of his adoption.   The utter absence of ostentation, and
the singleness of purpose which has characterized this bestowal o
many millions, render the act unique in the records of public benefactions.   Many wealthy persons have, in the evening of their days,
"when the grasshopper became a burden," or by will after death, be-
stowed large portions of their wealth for the public benefit; but in this
case, the donor is a man scarcely past the prime of life, in robust
health and the full strength of unimpaired faculties, surrounded by
everything which can make life pleasurable and with the prospect of
many years of enjoyment yet before him; a man who, by almost super-
human energy, enterprise and sagacity has amassed a vast fortune,
yet freely and voluntarily donates a large portion of his more than
princely wealth to advance the cause of education and afford the sons
and daughters of California ample opportunity for obtaining the
highest and broadest culture.   By this act Senator Stanford will not
only immortalize the memory of his son, but will erect for himself a
monument more enduring than brass or marble, for it will be en-
shrined in the hearts of succeeding generations for all time to come.
The Senator's idea is to make this a training school for the hand as
well as the center of intellectual culture, and from the manual labor
departments we anticipate the earliest and most practical benefits of
this great enterprise.

     In preparing the Endowment Act, passed by the last Legislature to
protect endowments of this character, the clearness of mind and intellectual power of Senator Stanford is fully demonstrated.   The decis-
ion rendered by Judge McKinstry, in the Hinckley estate litigation,
some two years ago, suggested to the Senator the absolute necessity of
a law to protect institutions receiving endowments.   He accordingly
prepared with his own hand the following Act, which, in all its details,
is admirably adapted to the purpose he had in view :

THE ENDOWMENT ACT

PROVISIONS UNDER WHICH THE GRANT IS MADE

*An act to advance learning, the arts and sciences, and to promote the pub-
lic welfare, by providing for the conveyance, holding and protection of
property, and the creation of trusts for the founding, endowment, erec-*

JAMES McMILLAN SHAFTER

tion and maintenance within this State of universities, colleges, schools,
seminaries of learning, mechanical institutes, museums and galleries
of art.

[Approved March 9, 1885.]

The people of the State of California, represented in Senate and
Assembly, do enact as follows:

SECTION 1. The provisions of this Act shall be liberally construed
with a view to effect its objects and promote its purposes; and in the
construction thereof the singular number shall be deemed to include
the plural, and the plural shall be deemed to include the singular
number, and the masculine gender shall be deemed to include the
feminine.

SEC. 2. Any person desiring, in his lifetime, to promote the public
welfare by founding, endowing and having maintained, within this
State, a university, college, school, seminary of learning, mechanical
institute, museum, or gallery of art, or any or all thereof, may, to
that end, and for such purpose, by grant in writing, convey to a
Trustee, or any number of Trustees named in such grant, (and to
their successors), any property, real or personal, belonging to such
person, and situated or being within this State; provided, that if any
such person be married and the property be community property,
then both husband and wife must join in such grant.

SEC. 3. The person making such grant may therein designate:

1. The nature, object and purposes of the institution or institutions
to be founded, endowed and maintained.

2. The name by which it or they shall be known.

3. The powers and duties of the Trustees, and the manner in
which they shall account, and to whom, if accounting be required;
but such powers and duties shall not be held to be exclusive of other
powers and duties which may be necessary to enable such Trustees to
fully carry out the objects of such grant.

4. The mode and manner, and by whom, the successors to the
Trustee or Trustees named in the grant are to be appointed.

5. Such rules and regulations for the management of the property
conveyed as the grantor may elect to prescribe; but such rules shall,
unless the grantor otherwise prescribe, be deemed advisory only, and
shall not preclude such Trustees from making such changes as new
conditions may, from time to time, require.

CHARLES GOODALL

6. The place or places where, and the time when, the buildings necessary and proper for the institution or institutions shall be erected, and the character and extent thereof. The person making such grant may therein provide for all other things necessary and proper to carry out the purposes thereof, and especially may such person provide for the trades and professions which shall be taught in such institutions, and the terms upon which deserving scholars of the public and private schools of the various counties of this State may be admitted to all the privileges of such institutions, as a reward for meritorious conduct and good scholarship; and also for maintaining free scholarships for children of persons who have rendered service to or who have died in the service of this State; and also for maintaining free scholarships for children of mechanics, tradesmen and laborers, who have died without leaving means sufficient to give such children a practical education, fitting them for the useful trades or arts; and also the terms and conditions upon which students in the public and private schools, and other deserving persons, may, without cost to themselves, attend the lectures of any university established; and also the terms and conditions upon which the museums, and art galleries, and conservatories of music, connected with any such institution, shall be open to all deserving persons, without charge, and without their becoming students of the institution.

Sec. 4. The Trustee or Trustees named in such grant, and their successors, may, in the name of the institution or institutions, as designated in such grant, sue and defend, in relation to the trust property, and in relation to all matters affecting the institution or institutions endowed and established by such grant.

Sec. 5. The person making such grant, by a provision therein, may elect, in relation to the property conveyed and in relation to the erection, maintenance and management of such institution or institutions, to perform, during his life, all the duties and exercise all the powers which, by the terms of the grant, are enjoined upon and vested in the Trustee or Trustees therein named. If the person making such grant, and making the election aforesaid, be a married person, such person may further provide that if the wife of such person survive him, then such wife, during her life, may, in relation to the property conveyed, and in relation to the erection, maintenance, and management of such institution or institutions, perform all the duties and exercise all the powers which, by the terms of the grant, are en-

ALFRED L. TUBBS

joined upon and vested in the Trustee or Trustees therein named, and in all such cases the powers and duties conferred and imposed by such grant upon the Trustee or Trustees therein named, shall be exercised and performed by the person making such grant, or by his wife during his or her life, as the case may be; provided, however, that upon the death of such person, or his surviving wife, as the case may be, such powers and duties shall devolve upon and shall be exercised by the Trustees named in the grant and their successors.

SEC. 6. The person making such grant may therein reserve the right to alter, amend or modify the terms and conditions thereof and the trusts therein created, in respect to any of the matters mentioned or referred to in subdivisions one to six inclusive, of section 2 hereof; and may also therein reserve the right, during the life of such person or persons, of absolute dominion over the personal property conveyed, and also over the rents, issues, and profits of the real property conveyed, without liability to account therefor in any manner whatever and without any liability over against the estate of such person; and if any such person be married, such person may, in said grant, further provide that if his wife survive him, then such wife, during her life, may have the same absolute dominion over such personal property, and such rents, issues and profits, without liability to account therefor in any manner whatever, and without liability over against the estate of either of the spouses.

SEC. 7. The person making such grant may therein provide that the Trustees named in the grant, and their successors, may in the name of the institution or institutions, become the custodian of the persons of minors, and when any such provision is made in a grant, the Trustees and their successors may take such custody and control in the manner and for the time, and in accordance with the provisions of sections two hundred and sixty-four to two hundred and seventy-six, inclusive, of the Civil Code of the State of California.

SEC. 8. Any such grant may be executed, acknowledged and recorded in the same manner as is now provided by law for the execution, acknowledgment and recording of grants of real property.

SEC. 9. No suit, action, or proceeding shall be commenced or maintained by any person to set aside, annul, or affect said conveyance, or to affect the title to the property conveyed, or the right to the possession, or to the rents, issues and profits thereof, unless the same be commenced within two years after the date of filing such

FRANCIS E. SPENCER

grant for record; nor shall any defence be made to any suit, action or proceedings commenced by the Trustee or Trustees named in said grant, or their successors, privies or persons holding under them, which defence involves the legality of said grant, or affects the title to the property thereby conveyed, or the right to the possession, or the rents, issues and profits thereof, unless such defence is made in a suit, action or proceeding commenced within two years after such grant shall have been filed for record.

SEC. 10.   The property conveyed by such grant shall not, after the lapse of two years from the date of the filling for record of the grant, be subject to forced sale under execution, or judical proceedings of any kind, against the grantor or his privies, unless the action under which the execution shall be issued, or the proceedings under which the sale shall be ordered, shall have been commenced within two years after such grant shall have been filed for record.   Nor shall such property be subject to execution or forced sale under any judgment obtained in any proceedings instituted within said two years, if there be other property of the grantor subject to execution or forced sale sufficient to satisfy such judgment, *provided*, nothing in this section contained shall be construed to affect mechanics' or laborers' liens.

SEC. 11.   Any person or persons making any such grant may, at any time thereafter, by last will or testament, devise and bequeath to the State of California all or any of the property, real and personal, mentioned in such grant, or in any supplemental grant, and such devise or bequest shall only take effect in case, from any cause whatever, the grant shall be annulled, or set aside, or the trusts therein declared shall for any reason fail.   Such devise and bequest is hereby permitted to be made by way of assurance that the wishes of the grantor or grantors shall be carried out, and in the faith that the State, in case it succeeds to the property, or any part thereof, will, to the extent and value of such property, carry out, in respect to the objects and purposes of any such grant, all the wishes and intentions of the grantor or grantors; *provided*, that no wish, direction, act or condition expressed, made, or given by any grantor or grantors, under or by virtue of this act, as to religious instruction to be given in such school, college, seminary, mechanical institute, museum or gallery of art, or in respect to the exercise of religious belief, on the part of any pupil or pupils of such school or institution of learning, shall be binding

HENRY VROOMAN

upon the State; nor shall the State enforce, or permit to be enforced or carried out, any such wish, direction, act, or condition.

SEC. 12.   This Act shall be in force from and after its passage.

After the passage of the foregoing Act, Senator Stanford completed his arrangements for the establishment and endowment of the Leland Stanford Junior University.   Twenty-four Trustees were appointed, viz. :

TRUSTEES

LORENZO SAWYER, one of the presiding Judges of the United States Circuit Court, San Francisco.

JAMES McM. SHAFTER, San Francisco, lawyer, formerly State Senator, and ex-President of the State Agricultural Society.

CHARLES GOODALL, San Francisco, of the Pacific Coast Steamship Company, formerly a Representative of San Francisco in the Legislature.

ALFRED L. TUBBS, merchant, St. Helena, Napa county, formerly a Senator from San Francisco.

FRANCIS E. SPENCER, Judge of the Superior Court, San Jose, and formerly a Representative from Santa Clara county in the Assembly.

HENRY VROOMAN, lawyer and State Senator from Alameda county.

CHARLES F. CROCKER, San Francisco, Vice-President of the Southern Pacific Railroad Company.

TIMOTHY HOPKINS, San Francisco, Treasurer of the Southern Pacific Railroad Company.

HENRY L. DODGE, San Francisco, merchant, formerly a State Senator from San Francisco and ex-Superintendent of the Mint.

IRVING M. SCOTT, San Francisco, of the Union Iron Works.

WILLIAM ASHBURNER, San Francisco, Regent of the State University.

Dr. H. W. HARKNESS, San Francisco, of the San Francisco Academy of Sciences.

JOSIAH STANFORD, viticulturist, Warm Springs, Alameda county.

HORACE DAVIS, merchant, San Francisco, ex-member of Congress from San Francisco.

JOHN F. MILLER, Napa, United States Senator from California (since deceased.)

JOHN BOGGS, farmer, Colusa, formerly State Senator from Colusa, a Director of the State Agricultural Society and of the Board of Prison Directors of the State.

CHARLES F. CROCKER

Hon. T. B. MCFARLAND, Sacramento, formerly in the Legislature of the State from Nevada county, and at present a Judge of the Superior Court of Sacramento.

ISAAC S. BELCHER, Marysville, formerly of the Supreme Bench of California.

JOHN Q. BROWN, Sacramento, Mayor of Sacramento.

GEORGE E. GRAY, San Francisco, ex-Chief Engineer of the Southern Pacific Railroad Company.

N. W. SPAULDING, Oakland, manufacturer and ex-United States Sub-Treasurer, and Grand Treasurer of the Grand Lodge of Free and Accepted Masons of California.

MATTHEW P. DEADY, Portland, Oregon, presiding Judge of the United States Circuit Court of Oregon.

WILLIAM M. STEWART, Virginia City, Nevada, ex-United States Senator from Nevada.

STEPHEN J. FIELD, Washington, D. C., Justice of the Supreme Court of the United States.

On the fourteenth day of November, 1885, a meeting of the Trustees was called at the residence of Senator Stanford, and all were present except James McM. Shafter, Matthew P. Deady, John F. Miller, and Stephen J. Field. The meeting was called to order, and upon motion Judge Lorenzo Sawyer was chosen Chairman of the Board of Trustees, and H. C. Nash was appointed Secretary, *pro tem.*

Col. Creed Haymond, addressing the gentlemen named in the deed of trust, said: "On the 11th of this month Governor Stanford and his wife made and executed a grant for the purpose of founding and endowing a university at Palo Alto, and you, gentlemen, among others, were named as the Trustees in that grant, and have been called together by Governor Stanford, in order that you may hear the grant read and receive delivery thereof, and at the request of Governor Stanford, if it meets with your approval, I will read the grant."

Creed Haymond then read the deed of Trust, which had been engrossed in a huge volume of parchment, in the old illustrated style, and is as follows:

TIMOTHY HOPKINS

GRANT FOUNDING AND ENDOWING THE LELAND STANFORD JUNIOR
UNIVERSITY

We, Leland Stanford, and Jane Lathrop Stanford, husband and
wife, grantors, desiring to promote the public welfare by founding,
endowing and having maintained upon our estate known as the Palo
Alto farm, and situated in the counties of San Mateo and Santa Clara,
State of California, United States of America, a university for both
sexes, with the colleges, schools, seminaries of learning, mechanical
institutes, museums, galleries of art, and all other things necessary
and appropriate to a university of high degree, to that end and for that
purpose do hereby grant, bargain, sell and convey to Lorenzo Sawyer,
James McM. Shafter, Charles Goodall, Alfred L. Tubbs, Francis E.
Spencer, Henry Vrooman, Charles F. Crocker, Timothy Hopkins,
Henry L. Dodge, Irving M. Scott, William Ashburner, H. W. Hark-
ness, Josiah Stanford, Horace Davis, John F. Miller, John Boggs, T.
B. McFarland, Isaac S. Belcher, John Q. Brown, George E. Gray, N.
W. Spaulding, of California; Matthew P. Deady, of Oregon; William
M. Stewart, of Nevada, and Stephen J. Field, a Justice of the Supreme
Court of the United States—Trustees, and to their successors forever,
all and singular the following described real property:

That certain tract of land situated in the county of Butte, State of
California, and now commonly known and designated as Stanford's
Gridley Farm.

Also that certain tract of land situated partly in the said county of
Butte and partly in the county of Tehama, in said State, and now
commonly known and designated as Stanford's Vina Farm.

And also that certain tract of land situated partly in the county of
Santa Clara and partly in the county of San Mateo, and now commonly known and designated as the Palo Alto Farm.

Together with all the tenements, hereditaments and appurtenances
thereunto belonging, with the water rights, water ditches, pipes,
flumes, canals, aqueducts and reservoirs now used in connection with
either of said tracts of land ; said tracts of land being more particu-
larly described by metes and bounds in the paper hereto attached,
marked "Schedule A," and made part thereof.

To have and to hold said property, and all other property, real and
personal, which we, or either of us, may hereafter convey or devise
to them or their successors upon the trust that it shall constitute the

THE LATE SENATOR JOHN F. MILLER

foundation and endowment for the University herein provided, and upon the trust that the principal thereof shall forever remain intact, and that the rents, issues and profits thereof shall be devoted to the foundation and maintenance of the University hereby founded and endowed, and to the uses and purposes herein mentioned.

Now, therefore, further, in pursuance of said desire, and that the trust hereby created may be executed according to the wishes of the grantors and each of them, they do hereby designate, as it is provided may be done by the Act of the Legislature of the State of California, approved March 9th, 1885, entitled "an Act to advance learning, the arts and sciences, and to promote the public welfare, by providing for the conveyance, holding and protection of property, and the creation of trusts for the founding, endowment, erection and maintenance within this State of universities, colleges, schools, seminaries of learning, mechanical institutes, museums and galleries of art," designate—

I.

THE NATURE, OBJECT AND PURPOSES OF THE INSTITUTION HEREBY FOUNDED, TO BE :

Its nature, that of a University with such seminaries of learning as shall make it of the highest grade, including mechanical institutes, museums, galleries of art, laboratories and conservatories, together with all things necessary for the study of agriculture in all its branches, and for mechanical training, and the studies and exercises directed to the cultivation and enlargement of the mind ;

Its object, to qualify students for personal success and direct usefulness in life.

And its purposes, to promote the public welfare by exercising an influence in behalf of humanity and civilization, teaching the blessings of liberty regulated by law, and inculcating love and reverence for the great principles of government as derived from the inalienable rights of man to life, liberty and the pursuit of happiness.

II.

THE NAME OF THE INSTITUTION.

Since the idea of establishing an institution of this kind for the benefit of mankind came directly and largely from our son and only

IRVING M. SCOTT

child, Leland, and in the belief that had he been spared to advise us
as to the disposition of our estate, he would have desired the devotion
of a large portion thereof to this purpose, we will that for all time to
come the institution hereby founded shall bear his name, and shall
be known as "The Leland Stanford Junior University."

III.

THE NUMBER, QUORUM AND DESIGNATION OF THE TRUSTEES.

The number of Trustees shall be twenty-four, and fifteen thereof
shall constitute a quorum, but the assent of not less than a majority
of the whole, to wit, thirteen, shall be necessary for affirmative action
in the execution of the trusts herein contained.

The Trustees herein named, and their successors, in their collective
capacity, shall be known and designated as "The Board of Trustees of
the Leland Stanford Junior University."

IV.

THAT THE TRUSTEES (SUBJECT TO THE RESERVATIONS AND TO THE RIGHTS TO ALTER AND AMEND HEREINAFTER CONTAINED) SHALL HAVE POWER AND IT SHALL BE THEIR DUTY:

1. To meet in the city of San Francisco on the 14th day of November, 1885, or as soon thereafter as pract cable, and then and there
—a majority of their number being present—to organize as a board
by selecting one of their number chairman, and to transact such other
business as may be proper.

2. To manage and control the institution hereby founded.

3. To manage and control the trust property, care for and improve
the same, operate or lease it, and apply the net proceeds or profits
thereof to the purposes of the trust hereby created.

4. To, in their discretion, receive grants of property from others
in aid of the institution founded, or to establish scholarships therein,
providing the same are made upon terms and conditions in harmony
with the purposes of the institution as herein declared.

5. To receive from the grantors, or either of them, by grant or
devise, such other property as the grantors or either of them may
hereafter elect to give, and to hold such property upon the same conditions, and to give the same uses and trusts as herein prescribed.

WILLIAM ASHBURNER

6. To make by-laws not inconsistent with the laws of this State, or the purposes of this grant, for the government of the institution hereby founded.

7. To makes rules and regulations for the management of the trust property.

8. To keep a full and fair record of their proceedings.

9. To appoint a President of the University, who shall not be one of their number, and to remove him at will.

10. To employ professors and teachers at the University.

11. To fix the salaries of the president, professors and teachers, and to fix them at such rates as will secure to the University the services of men of the very highest attainments.

12. To use the rents, issues and profits of the trust property (but no part of the principal), in the execution of their trust, and in case such rents, issues and profits, for any one year, exceed the amount necessary to execute the trust and maintain the institution for said year, then to invest the same until its use becomes necessary.

13. To establish and maintain at such University an educational system which will, if followed, fit the graduate for some useful pursuit, and to this end to cause the pupils, as early as may be, to declare the particular calling, which, in life, they may desire to pursue, but such declaration shall not be binding if, in the judgment of the President of the University, the student is not by nature fitted for the pursuit declared.

14. To prohibit sectarian instruction, but to have taught in the University the immortality of the soul, the existence of an all-wise and benevolent Creator, and that obedience to His laws is the highest duty of man.

15. To have taught in the University the right and advantages of association and co-operation.

16. To afford equal facilities and give equal advantages in the University to both sexes.

17. To maintain on the Palo Alto estate a farm for instruction in agriculture in all its branches.

18. To do and perform all things hereinafter provided for, and all things necessary to the proper exercise and discharge of their trust.

MATTHEW P. DEADY, OF OREGON

V.

THE POWERS AND DUTIES OF THE PRESIDENT OF THE UNIVERSITY.

It shall be the duty of the Trustees to give to the President of the University the following powers :

1. To prescribe the duties of the professors and teachers.

2. To remove professors and teachers at will.

3. To prescribe and enforce the course of study and the mode and manner of teaching.

4. Such other powers as will enable him to control the educational part of the University to such an extent that he may *justly be* held responsible for the course of study therein, and for the good conduct and capacity of the professors and teachers.

VI.

THE FACULTY.

The Trustees shall constitute the President and Professors the Faculty of the University, and prescribe their powers and duties as such.

VII.

THE MANNER, AND TO WHOM, THE TRUSTEES SHALL REPORT.

The Board of Trustees shall annually report all their proceedings to the person who, for the time being, shall fill the office of Governor of the State of California, and shall accompany such report with a full account of their financial operations for the preceding year, and with a statement of the financial affairs of the institution.

VIII.

THE MODE AND MANNER, AND BY WHOM, THE SUCCESSORS TO THE TRUSTEES NAMED IN THE GRANT ARE TO BE APPOINTED.

Any trustee named in this grant, or the successor to any Trustee, may for good cause be removed by a proper court of equity jurisdiction, after notice to him, and upon the application of the grantors herein, or either of them, or upon the application of the Board of Trustees.

Any trustee named in this grant, or the successor of any such Trustee, may, in writing, addressed and delivered to the Board of

H. W. HARKNESS

Trustees, resign his office as Trustee, and every vacancy in the Trustees which shall occur during the lives of the grantors, or during the life of either of them, either from the failure of any Trustee named in this grant to accept the trust, or from death, resignation or otherwise, shall be filled by the grantors, or either of them, as the case may be, and every vacancy occurring thereafter shall be filled by the surviving or remaining Trustees, by ballot.

IX.

THE PLACE WHERE, AND THE TIME WHEN, THE BUILDINGS NECESSARY AND PROPER FOR THE INSTITUTION SHALL BE ERECTED; THE CHARACTER AND EXTENT THEREOF.

The Trustees shall :

1. Within two years from the date hereof, select and lay off on the Palo Alto farm a site, and adopt a general plan for the construction of the University buildings. Such buildings shall be plain and substantial in character and extensive enough to provide accommodations for the University, and the colleges, schools, seminaries, mechanical institutes, museums, laboratories, conservatories and galleries of art, part thereof. They shall be built as needed, and not faster, and in a manner which shall allow for additions and extensions from time to time, as the necessities of the University may demand, the Trustees bearing in mind that extensive and expensive buildings do not make a University ; that it depends for its success rather upon the character and attainments of its faculty. In this behalf, and to the end that the endowment may not be wasted or impaired by the premature construction of expensive buildings, the Trustees shall be the exclusive judges, free from all interference from any source whatever, of the time when buildings are needed, and of the time and manner of their construction, and of the time and manner of making additions thereto.

2. Lay off on the Palo Alto farm one or more sites for buildings for the officers and employees of the institution, and erect and maintain thereon such buildings as may be necessary.

3. Lay off on the Palo Alto farm one or more sites for dwelling houses for parents or guardians and their families, and for such other persons as the board may direct, and erect thereon buildings and

JOSIAH STANFORD

lease the same, or lease the land and permit the lessees to erect such buildings, on such terms and conditions as the board may direct.

4. Lay off on said Palo Alto farm a lot of about ten acres, and suitably improve and maintain the same forever as a place of burial and of last rest on earth for the bodies of the grantors and of their son Leland Stanford, Junior, and as the board may direct, for the bodies of such other persons, who may have been connected with the University.

5. Lay off on the Palo Alto farm a site for, and erect thereon, a church.

X.

THE SCHOLARSHIPS AND OTHER MATTERS CONNECTED THEREWITH.

The Trustees shall have power, and it shall be their duty :

1. To establish and maintain, in connection with the University, such a number of free scholarships as the endowment of the institution, considering all its objects, will justify. Such scholarships must be given either to those who, by good conduct and study, have earned the right thereto, or to the deserving children of those who, dying without means in the service of the State, or in the cause of humanity, have a special claim upon the good-will of mankind.

2. To fix the terms and conditions upon which the students generally may be admitted to all or any of the privileges of the University.

3. To fix the terms and conditions upon which the students of the public and private schools and other deserving persons may attend the lectures of the University, or engage in original research thereat, and the terms and conditions upon which the agricultural farms, laboratories, museums, art galleries, mechanical institutes, conservatories and other institutions, part of the University, shall be open to deserving persons, without their becoming students thereof.

4. To establish and have given at the University, by its ablest professors, courses of lectures upon the science of government, and upon law, medicine, mechanics and the other arts and sciences, which shall be free to the post-graduates of the colleges of the University hereby founded, and to the post-graduates of all other colleges and universities, and to all deserving persons, to the full capacity of the lecture rooms, under such rules and regulations as the Trustees may adopt.

HORACE DAVIS

XI.

ELECTION OF THE GRANTORS TO CONTROL THE PROPERTY
AND THE EXECUTION OF THE TRUST DURING THEIR
LIVES, OR THE LIFE OF EITHER.

The grantors, and each of them, do hereby, in accordance with the provisions of the aforesaid Act of the Legislature, elect :

1. In relation to the property hereby conveyed, and in relation to such other property as may hereafter be conveyed or devised by them or either of them to said Trustees for the purpose of this trust, and in relation to the erection, maintenance and management of the institution hereby founded to perform during their lives all the duties and exercise all the powers and privileges which, by the terms of this grant, are enjoined upon and vested in the Trustees therein named.

2. That the survivor of either of said grantors shall, after the death of the other, and during the life of the survivor, in relation to all of said property, and in relation to the erection, maintenance and management of the institution hereby founded, perform all the duties and exercise all the powers and privileges which, by the terms of this grant, are enjoined and vested in the Trustees therein named.

3. That upon the death of both grantors, then all such duties shall devolve upon, and all such powers and privileges shall be exercised by, the Trustees named in this grand, and by their successors for ever.

XII.

RESERVATION OF THE RIGHT TO ALTER, AMEND OR MODIFY
THE TERMS AND CONDITIONS OF THIS GRANT, AND THE
TRUST THEREIN CREATED, IN CERTAIN RESPECTS.

The grantors hereby reserve to themselves, during their lives, and hereby reserve and grant to the one who shall survive the other, during his or her life, the right to alter, amend or modify the terms and conditions of this grant, and the trust therein created, in respect to the nature, objects and purposes of the institution founded, the powers and duties of the Trustees ; the manner in which, and to whom, they shall account ; the mode and manner, and by whom, their successors shall be appointed ; the rules and regulations for the management of the property conveyed ; the time when, and the character and extent of, the buildings which shall be erected ; the right to pro-

HENRY LEE DODGE

vide for trades and professions which shall be taught in the institution, and the terms upon which scholarships shall be founded.

XIII.

RESERVATION OF OTHER RIGHTS.

The grantors hereby reserve to themselves during their lives, and hereby reserve and grant to the one who shall survive the other, during his or her life:

1. The right to absolute dominion over the personal property, which they, or either of them, may hereafter give to said Trustees, or their successors, and over the rents, issues, and profits thereof.

2. The right to absolute dominion over the rents, issues, and profits of the real property hereby granted.

3. The right to improve, manage and control the trust property, as if this trust had not been made ; but this reservation does not include the right or power to sell or encumber any of the real property granted.

All these rights, and all other rights reserved by and all powers and privileges given, or duties imposed upon, the grantors, or either of them, by the terms of this grant, shall be exercised, enjoyed and performed by said grantors, or either of them, as the case may be, without let or hindrance, and free from all interference from any source whatever, and from all duty to report their action, and from all liability to account in any manner therefor, and from all liability for waste, loss, misappropriation, or for any act or deed whatever, by them or either of them done or permitted.

XIV.

THE CUSTODY OF THE PERSONS OF MINORS.

And further, in pursuance of said desire, the grantors hereby provide that the Trustees named in this grant, and their successors, may, in the name of the institution, become the custodian of the persons of minors, taking such custody in the manner, and for the time, and in accordance with the provisions of sections 264 to 275, inclusive, of the Civil Code of the State of California.

JOHN BOGGS

XV.

LIMITATIONS UPON THE POWERS OF THE TRUSTEES.

1. Neither of the Trustees herein named, nor their successors, shall have power to sell or convey the real property hereinbefore described and granted.

2. The Trustees herein named, and their successors, shall serve without compensation.

XVI.

MISCELLANEOUS.

The grantors hereby declare :

1. That all the property hereby conveyed was acquired by them during coverture, and was, until this grant was executed, their community property, and for that reason, and because of their mutual desire to be associated in this undertaking, they, in accordance with the provisions of the aforesaid Act of the Legislature, have joined in this conveyance.

2. This grant, and all grants and devises hereafter made by the grantors or either of them for endowing and maintaining the institution hereby founded, shall be liberally construed, and always with a view to effect the objects and promote the purposes of the grantors, as herein expressed.

In testimony whereof, the said Leland Stanford and Jane Lathrop Stanford, his beloved wife, have hereunto set their hands and affixed their seals, at the city and county of San Francisco, State of California, United States of America, this 11th day of November, in the year of our Lord and Savior, one thousand eight hundred and eighty-five.

LELAND STANFORD,
JANE LATHROP STANFORD.

In the presence of Stephen T. Gage, E. H. Miller, Jr., Nicholas T. Smith, Herbert C. Nash and Creed Haymond.

STATE OF CALIFORNIA,   } ss.
City and County of San Francisco.

On this 11th day of November, A. D. one thousand eight hundred and eighty-five, before me, Holland Smith, a Notary Public in and for said city and county, duly qualified and acting as such, personally

T. B. McFARLAND

appeared Leland Stanford, known to me to be one of the persons whose name is subscribed to the foregoing instrument, and acknowledged to me that he executed the same.

In witness whereof, I have hereunto set may hand and affixed my official seal, at my office, in the city and county of San Francisco, the day and year last above written.

HOLLAND SMITH, Notary Public.

307 Montgomery street.

STATE OF CALIFORNIA,   }
City and County of San Francisco.} ss.

On this 11th day of November, A. D. one thousand eight hundred and eighty-five, before me, Holland Smith, a Notary Public in and for said city and county, duly qualified and acting as such, personally appeared Jane Lathrop Stanford, known to me to be the person whose name is subscribed to the foregoing instrument, and therein described as a married woman, and, upon an examination without the hearing of her husband, I made her acquainted with the contents of said instrument, and thereupon she acknowledged to me that she executed the same, and that she does not wish to retract such execution.

In witness whereof, I have hereunto set my hand and affixed my official seal, at my office in the city and county of San Francisco, the day and year last above written.

HOLLAND SMITH, Notary Public.

307 Montgomery street.

After Colonel Haymond concluded the reading of the grant, Senator Stanford arose, and addressed the Trustees as follows:

Gentlemen: In the trust deed providing for the endowment and organization of the University, the nature, objects, and purposes of the endowment are very generally stated.   We deem it appropriate, however, to enlarge somewhat upon what is therein set forth.

The reasons that impelled us to select the Palo Alto estate as the location for the University, are its personal associations, which are most dear to us, the excellence of its climate, and its accessibility.

The deed of trust conveys, and at once irrevocably vests in you, the title to all the real property described therein.

The endowment of lands is made because they are, in themselves, of great value, and their proper management will insure to the University an income much greater than would be realized were their

ISAAC SAWYER BELCHER

value to be invested in any reliable, interest-bearing security. Again, they can never be alienated, and will, therefore, be an unfailing support to the institution which they are designated to benefit.

As a further assurance that the endowment will be ample to establish and maintain a University of the highest grade, we have, by last will and testament, devised to you and your successors additional property. We have done this as a security against the uncertainties of life, and in the hope that during our lives the full endowment may go to you. With this in view, we have provided in this grant that you may take such other property as we may give to more fully carry out the objects of this trust.

The Palo Alto farm furnishes a sufficiently diversified soil, with a topography which admirably fits it as a place for agricultural education. In time, also, a handsome income will be derived from the rental of desirable residences to parents and others who will choose the place as a residence on account of its social, intellectual, and climatic advantages. Of course, the Trustees will see to it that no objectionable people are allowed to reside upon the estate, and that no drinking saloons shall ever be opened upon any part of the premises.

BROAD AND GENERAL IDEAS OF PROGRESS.

It should be the aim of the institution to entertain and inculcate broad and general ideas of progress and of the capacity of mankind for advancement in civilization. It is clear that to insure the steady advancement of civilization great care must be exercised in the matter of the general development of the great body of the people. They need education in the fundamental principles of government, and we know of no text so plain and so suggestive as that clause in our Declaration of Independence which declares that "Among the inalienable rights of man are life, liberty, and the pursuit of happiness, and that to secure these rights governments are instituted among men, deriving their just powers from the consent of the governed."

A government founded on such principles commands for the support and protection of individual rights the force of the whole people. With these principles fully recognized, agrarianism and communism can have only an ephemeral existence.

The merely physical wants of civilized man are not much greater than those of the savage, but his intellectual wants are bounded only by his capacity to conceive. His wants, therefore, will always depend

JOHN Q. BROWN

upon his advancement in civilization, and the demand for labor will be measured accordingly. The rapidity of the communication of modern thought and the facilities of transportation make the civilized world one great neighborhood, in whose markets all producers meet in competition. The relative compensation to the producer must depend upon his powers of production.

DESIRES OF CIVILIZED SOCIETY.

When we consider the endless variety of the wants and the desires of civilized society, we must fully appreciate the value of labor-aiding machinery and the necessity for having this of the best character. Too much attention, therefore, cannot be given to technical and mechanical instruction to the end that from our institution may go out educators in every field of production.

Out of these suggestions grows the consideration of the great advantages, especially to the laboring man, of co-operation, by which each individual has the benefit of the intellectual and physical forces of his associates. It is by the intelligent application of these principles that there will be found the greatest lever to elevate the mass of humanity, and laws should be formed to protect and develop co-operative associations. Laws with this object in view will furnish to the poor man complete protection against the monopoly of the rich, and such laws properly administered and availed of, will insure to the workers of the country the full fruits of their industry and enterprise. They will accomplish all that is sought to be secured by the labor-leagues, trades-unions, and other federations of workmen, and will be free from the objection of even implicitly attempting to take the unauthorized or wrongful control of the property, capital, or time of others.

Hence it is that we have provided for thorough instruction in the principles of co-operation. We would have it early instilled into the student's mind that no greater blow can be struck at labor than that which makes its products insecure.

ARTICLES OF ENDOWMENT.

While the articles of endowment prohibit sectarianism, they direct that there shall be taught that there is an all-wise, benevolent God and that the soul is immortal. It seems to us that the welfare of man on earth depends on the belief in immortality, and that the advan-

GEORGE EDWARD GRAY

tages of every good act and the disadvantages of every evil one, follow man from this life into the next, there attaching to him as certainly as individuality is maintained.

As to the manner in which this shall be taught and whence the confirmations shall be derived, we are not prepared to advance any thought other than that they may be sought from every available source that tends to throw light upon the subject.

While it is our desire that there shall be no sectarian teaching in this institution, it is very far from our thoughts to exclude divine service. We have provided that a suitable building be erected wherein the professors of the various religious denominations shall, from time to time, be invited to deliver discourses not sectarian in character.

We deem it of the first importance that the education of both sexes shall be equally full and complete, varied only as nature dictates. The *rights* of one sex, political and otherwise, are the same as those of the other sex, and this equality of rights ought to be fully recognized.

We have sought to place the free scholarships upon the basis of right to the student. We think this important, in order that his dignity and self-respect shall be maintained and that he may understand that in his political relations he is entitled to nothing he does not learn.

With respect to the expenses of the students of the University, we desire that the Trustees shall fix them as low as possible.

The articles of endowment are intended to be in the nature of a constitution for the government and guidance of the Board of Trustees, in a general manner, not in detail. We hope that this institution will endure through long ages. Provisions regarding details of management, however wise they may be at present, might prove to be mischievous under conditions which may arise in the future.

In the deed of trust we have designated the purposes of this University. The object is not alone to give the student a technical education, fitting him for a successful business life, but it is also to instill into his mind an appreciation of the blessings of this Government, a reverence for its institutions, and a love for God and humanity, to the end that he may go forth and by precept and example spread the great truths by the light of which his fellow man will be elevated and taught how to attain happiness in this world and in the life eternal.

NATHAN W. SPAULDING

THE GROWTH OF TIME.

We do not expect to establish a University and fill it with students at once. It must be the growth of time and experience. Our idea is that in the first instance we shall require the establishment of colleges for both sexes; then of primary schools, as they may be needed, and out of all these will grow the great central institution for more advanced study.

We have fixed the number of Trustees at twenty-four, that the institution may have the strength which comes from numbers. There is little danger of divided counsels, for the Educational Department will be under the control of the President of the University, who will have and exercise all the power necessary to make him responsible for its successful management. In order that he may have the assistance of a competent staff of professors we have provided that the best talent obtainable shall be procured and that liberal compensation shall always be offered.

We are impressed with the deep responsibilities of this undertaking and invoke at all times your aid and the Divine help and blessing. During our lives we hope that we shall be compelled to make little draft upon the time of you, gentlemen, members of the Board of Trustees of the Leland Stanford Junior University, yet we trust that you will be ever ready to assist us with your counsel.

THE TRUSTEES ACCEPT.

When Senator Stanford finished his address he said to the Trustees: "Gentlemen, I did not ask any of you in advance of the selection if you would serve as Trustees. I made the selection with the fullest belief in your fitness and integrity, and I hope you are all satisfied with your associates."

Upon motion of Judge Spencer, of San Jose, the following resolution was adopted:

"*Resolved,* That the Trustees receive said grant, and accept for themselves and their associates the trusts therein imposed."

All the trustees present then signed the original deed on parchment, and upon motion of Judge Sawyer, the following resolution was adopted:

"*Resolved,* That the Secretary be authorized for, and as the act and deed of the Trustees, to have the grant herein properly recorded on

WM. M. STEWART

the records of the counties of Tehama, Butte, San Mateo, and Santa Clara, State of California."

On motion of Mr. Vrooman, the Trustees then adjourned, to meet at the call of the Chairman.

Senator and Mrs. Stanford then invited the Trustees to lunch, which was spread in most elaborate style in an adjoining room.

During the entire proceedings, which lasted more than an hour, Senator Stanford displayed an utter unconsciousness of doing anything more than a simple act of patriotic duty. He was less impressed with the magnitude of the deed than anyone else, and gave his property away in such a simple, unostentatious manner that many of those present could not help remarking his complete self-abnegation. He intimated, during some informal talk, that his own and his wife's will had been made, and that in case of their death within a short period, they had made large additional bequests to carry out the plans respecting the Leland Stanford Junior University.

STANFORD'S AIMS. — SOME IDEA OF WHAT THE GREAT UNIVERSITY WILL BE WHEN COMPLETE.

The following, from the *Post*, conveys a clear idea of Senator Stanford's intentions relative to the University, and of the nature and value of the property conveyed :

The act by which Senator Stanford so grandly endowed the Palo Alto Institute of Learning will, in the years to come, rank as one of the great events in the history of the State of California, and, for that matter, the United States. Since the death of his only child, Leland Stanford, Jr., it has been the sole aim of the Senator's life to found an institution of learning in this State, which should be equal to all, and, if possible, excel, the best colleges in the world. To this end he draughted and secured the enactment last winter of a law for the protection of all endowments that may be made in the future for educational institutions in California. Since that time his attention has been largely paid to the perfection of his plans for the founding of the great educational center. By the deed of trust, which he placed in the hands of the trustees of the institute, he conveys for the lasting benefit of the institution 83,200 acres of land, comprising the most valuable estates in California, the products of which will go toward the fulfilment of his wishes. And at the same time, to guard against

STEPHEN J. FIELD

any possibility of failure of the plan by death or other unexpected events, Senator and Mrs. Stanford have made their wills, by which they provide for further vast endowments of the institution, which it is said will afford a greater income than can ever be utilized. This, however, is but a temporary expedient for the purpose of safety, for they hope to be able to put their property in such a shape that the whole endowment can be turned over to the trustees during their lives and that they may live to devote their whole time and attention to the completion and realization of their great project.

A GRAND CONCEPTION.

Those who are acquanted with the history of Senator Stanford, know that he never does a thing "by halves," yet the public can but be surprised when they learn of the wonderful work he has undertaken and the vast scope to be covered by this Palo Alto institution. It is his intention to make it a fount of learning that will satisfy the cravings of all classes for knowledge, from the commoner mechanical trades to the highest branches of art, science and mechanics—in fact, an educational center that will obviate the necessity which now compels the ambitious students of this country to go to Europe to complete their education.

There will be no branch of the arts, sciences or mechanics that will not be taught in Palo Alto, and to these educational advantages, male and female will be equally entitled. The institution by the munificent salaries it will be able to pay, will draw to its force of educators, the most famous and talented professors on the globe; and the splendid climate of the section of country in which Palo Alto is situated, will in no small degree, tend to induce the great professors of the East and Europe to accept chairs in its departments. The youth of California, and America as well, can now look forward to the time in the near future, when the doors of a free institution will be thrown open to them, wherein the highest standard of excellence in technical learning known to our civilization may be attained. The departments will include a college of medicine, which it will be the aim of Senator Stanford to make the greatest in this country and to the conduct of which, if possible, will be called such men as Jenner, of London, and Brown Sequard, of Paris, the lectures of whom the best physicians of America may attend with profit. There will be a college of law, presided over by the ablest masters of the law to be obtained; a department wherein

CREED HAYMOND

will be taught all the sciences and higher mathematics; a school of
arts, in which, under the ablest professors, such as now draw students
from all parts of the civilized world to Munich, thorough instruction
will be given in painting, sculpture, drawing, design, etc.

THE MUSICAL COLLEGE.

A grand conservatory of music, under the direction of the most
famous masters of Italy and Europe, which will afford the best musical
education to be had in the world, will be one of the particular features
of this institute of technics. There will also be a School of Mechanics,
which will turn out all grades in this class, from the common artisan
to the scientific civil engineer and master machinist, and include instruction in all grades of scientific draughting and architecture. One
of the important branches of the institution will be a School of Agriculture, to which will be attached a farm, the soil and climate of
which will produce any of the agricultural or horticultural products of
the temperate or semi-tropic zones. Among the valuable adjuncts of
the institution are to be a splendid museum and libraries, containing
the best works pertaining to the various departments of learning.
And this is not all. When the time comes, as it eventually will, that
Palo Alto becomes an educational center, around which will be built a
town, the intention of Senator Stanford is to erect buildings for pre-
paratory schools, in order that people residing there may have facilities
for educating their younger children up to the standard at which
pupils will be admitted to the higher courses.

The deed of trust carefully provides against expenditure of money
on buildings that may be useless as universities, the projector believing that the faculty is the element to be most considered. Senator
Stanford's idea is to have the buildings erected in the form of a
parallelogram, and it is intended that two colleges shall be built at
first—one for males and the other for females.

SITE FOR A LARGE TOWN.

These colleges, and all other buildings, will be constructed on a plan
admitting of expansion and additions whenever necessary. He has
also provided for selecting a site at Palo Alto, upon which are to be
erected buildings for the accommodation of parents and guardians of
children, and such other persons as the trustees may permit to reside
there. These buildings will be rented at a fair rental, the proceeds

to go to the fund for the support of the University. Following the erection of the two first colleges will be the building of institutions in which will be given the higher course of education. These colleges will be provided with ample lecture rooms, and a provision of the deed of trust requires the trustees to pay the highest salaries for instructors of any institution of the kind in the world. This higher course will be free to post-graduates of all colleges and universities, and to such other deserving persons as the trustees may elect to admit. Free scholarships will be established in the colleges of the University, which are to be given to deserving pupils of the public schools, or to the children of those who have died without means, in the service of the State or the cause of humanity. The trustees will deal with the property chiefly. They will elect the President of the University and appoint the professors and teachers, but the President will have charge of the course of study, as to what it shall include and he will also have the power to discharge any teacher or professor at any time, thereby making him directly responsible to the trustees for the educational management of the institution. It is the Senator's idea to make the President absolute, with the other members of the faculty as his staff, believing that responsibility and power belong together. At a certain stage of his progress, each student will be required to select the pursuit he is to follow through life, and if the selection is approved by the President as practical, the pupil will be afforded every possible advantage to perfect himself or herself in the chosen calling.

A NOBLE BENEFACTOR.

Palo Alto is so near San Francisco and the University at Berkeley, that when the Southern Pacific Railroad is built along the bay shore, the run can be made from this city to Palo Alto in forty minutes without using any more power than is required at present, and the time will be eventually made much shorter. Low rates of fare will be given, for the purpose of encouraging attendance at the institution; and this will make Palo Alto a very desirable place of residence for people who have children to educate and who do business in this city. On the other hand, it will afford facilities for the children of people who reside here to attend the University and still live at home; and the same may be said of those persons who may desire to take the higher courses of study. With this incentive to settlement there, it will be but a short time ere Palo Alto will become in reality a suburb of San Francisco.

During their lives the University will be under the control of Senator and Mrs. Stanford, as they are named as Trustees, but the grant provides that they cannot sell or encumber the property in any way, and that it is devised forever. It was for this reason that Senator Stanford felt averse to going into the United States Senate, desiring to devote the remainder of his life exclusively to the institution he has founded, and to give it his care and the direction which he thinks it ought to have; but the senatorship came to him in such a manner that he felt he was not free to decline. Now that he has dedicated himself and a large portion of his property to the use of the State, his methods as a Senator will never be misunderstood, and he ought to be able to do a great deal for the State, of which for nearly a third of a century he has been a part.

The Palo Alto Estate.

The great estate of Palo Alto, with its magnificent distances, beautiful scenery, fruitful soil, rich productive powers and excellent location, forms one of the finest private properties in the United States. Unlike other large ranches in this State, it is not composed of a Spanish grant, but is the result of the consolidation of several farms into one, it being only recently that Senator Stanford bought a large property adjoining Palo Alto, and added it to the estate. With the exception of a few acres, the ranch lies wholly west of the Southern Pacific Railroad, a portion of it adjoining Menlo Park station, twenty miles from this city. On the eastern side runs the county highway from San Jose to San Francisco, and midway, east and west, that of Searsville and Mayfield. The first purchase was made in 1876, from Mr. Gordon, consisting of 800 acres. Since that time the following ranches have been acquired: Hoog, 800 acres; Martin, 982; Dixon, 1,700; Coutts, 1,400; Lieb, 1,200; scattering, 318; making a total of 7,200 acres. The soil consists of sandy loam, clay loam and adobe. A large portion of the land at the present time is used for pasture, but farming is carried on upon a large scale, under the direction of an able superintendent. This fine domain has an area of about eight miles north and south and six miles northeast by southwest. It is divided into four departments, known as the Trotting Horse department, the Running Horse department, the Farming department and the House and Grounds department; the latter embracing the park, vineyards and reservoir, the old vineyard containing forty acres and the young one sixty acres.

VALUABLE IMPROVEMENTS.

Near the mansion are the vegetable gardens, greenhouses, etc., and leading from it is the "Governor's avenue," a straight roadway lined with eucalyptus and walnut trees, leading through the heart of the ranch to the trotting farm. On the east of this road is a carrot field of sixty acres, these vegetables being raised for the entire stock of the farm. Adjoining it is a large cornfield and across the avenue a pasture in which the famous Occident and the favored horses of young Leland are exempted from further labors. Further on is a forty-acre alfalfa field and next to this a pasture of one hundred and twenty acres, in which are kept about one hundred weanlings of the herd. Where the avenue strikes the trotting farm is located the trotting park of sixty acres, containing two tracks, the outer one a mile and the inner three-quarters of a mile long. Besides shelter for spectators, here are situated the buildings comprising the quarters of the stock and the boarding house of the grooms and trainers. The tracks are kept in the most perfect condition, being rolled and sprinkled daily, and near them are miniature tracks in which the young horses are trained before being "broke" to harness. A system, peculiar to Governor Stanford, is used in training the young animals, which brings forth the best results possible, as shown by the wonderful records made by horses that have been raised on this farm. The trotting stud at present consists of ten full-aged stallions, fifty young stallions, two hundred and fifty brood mares, and about two hundred and fifty colts and fillies less than three years old. This year there have been one hundred and six foals. There are in constant training about ninety colts, each of which is exercised twenty minutes daily. Although there have never been any annual sales of stock, eighty-five thoroughbreds and trotters were disposed of last year. Behind the main course are covered training paddocks, and the main stable, one hundred and fifty feet long, with a fifty-five foot L., for the brood mares.

THE GREAT PALO ALTO SIRES.

On this portion of the ranch are kept the great stallions, such as Electioneer, Benton, Frolic, Clay, with a record of 2:25, and Piedmont, who cost $30,000 and has a record of 2:17½. In this department everything has been arranged so that with proper management a good revenue may be derived.

The thoroughbred farm, situated about two miles away, is composed of pasture grounds. On this farm are kept thirty brood mares and two stallions—Shannon and Flood—and about twenty colts in training for Eastern events covering the next two years. Among these brood mares are fifteen brought from England in 1884, which were sired by the best stallions in England—such as the Hermit, Salvator, Axminster, Pedro Gomez, Lowlander, Scottish Chief, North Lincoln, Adventurer, etc. The majority of them were imported with foal which was also sired by the finest stock. One is by Fiddler, the fastest stallion in England, and others are by Wemlock, Mask, Balf, Fetterlock, Isonomy, Foxhall, Peter, Macgregor and Peregrine, some of which are said to be the finest living stallions.

THE PARK AND GROUNDS

Portion of the ranch, which is situated at the entrance to Palo Alto, comprises 299 acres, and on this section more money has been expended for adornment than anywhere else. It was the Senator's intention to have the park contain every known species of tree that would grow in this climate, 12,000 trees having been added to the large collection last year. The scenery in this part of the estate is most beautiful, and nowhere in the land could there be found a more fitting site for a great institute of learning than here. On the Martin farm of 982 acres, it has been the Senator's intention to build a reservoir covering over 200 acres, to hold the waters of San Francisquito to the extent of 225,000,000 gallons. This reservoir would be expected to irrigate every portion of the ranch, excepting the foot-hills. A reservoir has already been constructed on the Mezes property, holding 125,000,000 gallons. On this ranch are foot-hills affording the finest wild oats pasturage, while the valleys contain the richest of farming land, especially adapted to the raising of barley.

FUTURE CULTIVATION.

Here also are kept about 100 fine brood mares. To the south-ward of this ranch lie 1,500 acres of hill, and, at this time, mostly unproductive. Many teams are now engaged in plowing, and the overseer promises to put 4,000 or 4,500 acres in cultivation the coming year. For the irrigation of portions of the ranch, besides the reservoir above mentioned, is one covering forty-five acres, and holding 35,090,000 gallons of water. There is also an artesian well on this ranch which has a capacity to funish 5,000 gallons per hour. This supplies water for all purposes for the home portion of the ranch.

For the conduct of this great estate one hundred and fifty persons are employed, at salaries ranging from $30 to $250 per month, of which number one hundred and four are white and the rest Chinese. The employees are all boarded by their employer. Church services are conducted on the place, and Mrs. Stanford has established a school for boys and a kindergarten for girls in Menlo Park. To sum up, Palo Alto is the largest horse farm in the world, and although it was never managed for profit, could undoubtedly be made to yield a large income. The total expense of running the ranch is about $225,000 per year, of which amount $90,000 is for wages. At the present time the actual income is about two-thirds of that amount, as follows : Vineyards, net, $10,000 yearly ; hay fields, 2,300 tons ; oats, 260,000 pounds ; barley, 240,000 pounds ; wheat, 100,000 pounds ; and rye, 70,000 pounds. The product of the 2,500 acres farmed in 1884 was $40,000.

Palo Alto also has a fine mansion, and all the luxuries of a beautiful manor.

The Vina Ranch.

The most valuable and productive of the three great ranches donated by Senator Stanford is the Vina Ranch, situated at the junction of Deer Creek with the Sacramento River, in Tehama County. It is a portion of an old Spanish grant made to Peder Lassen, a Swede, who settled upon it long before the discovery of gold in this State. Later it passed into the possession of a German named Gerke, who for many years made from its vineyard a brand of hock that was famous in the San Francisco markets. In 1881 the old man died, and Senator Stanford purchased the grant, adding to it other pieces of land, until he secured 55,000 acres, at a cost of $1,000,000. The old vineyard was "played out," the fences down, houses dilapidated, and there was no provision for irrigation.

In 1882, Senator Stanford ordered 1,000 acres set out to vineyard, and 800,000 cuttings were planted, comprising the finest varieties of wine, raisin, and table grapes, the first named predominating. The varieties are the Black Don, Burger, Black Burgundy, Hanstrillo, Charbonneau, Zinfandel, Black Elben, Black Malvoise, Nerdal, Trousseaux, Chargre, Poulsan, Lenoir, and Herbemont, to which have been added a number of other grafts especially imported from Europe. The Trousseau, Charbonneau, and Herbemont, are those principally used for port wine—the Zinfandel for claret and the Berger for white wine—the opinion being held on the ranch that this latter is to be the coming hock. In the following spring 1,500 acres more were set out, but in 1884 nothing was done in that line owing to the death of the lamented Leland Stanford, Jr. In the spring of the present year 1,000 acres more of vines were added, aggregating, with the seventy-five acres of the old Gerke vineyard, a total of 3,575 acres, or 2,860,-000 vines in one vineyard, making it by far the largest vineyard in the world, and some claim it to be larger than any three vineyards in the world combined. The whole 3,575 acres are laid out in blocks 152 feet in width by 552 feet in length, separated by alleys running north and south, and by avenues running east and west—the alleys 16 feet wide and the avenues forty-eight feet wide. These blocks lie along the Sacramento river and are parallel with the railroad, which runs through it from north to south. The avenues are lined on each side either with walnut, apricot, peach, plum, or other trees, and running through the center of each avenue is an irrigating ditch, 15 feet wide, with a 12-foot roadway on either side.

THE GREAT DIVISIONS.

The ranch is divided into two portions—agricultural and horticultural, the different sections or industries being allotted as follows: Vineyard, 3,575 acres ; alfalfa, 1,500 acres ; wheat, 3,000 acres ; orchard, 25 acres ; rental on shares, 2,500 acres ; in oat hay, 400 acres ; uncultivated bottom and timber land, 3,000 acres ; grazing land, plain and foot-hills, 41,000—total 55,000.

The preparations for the irrigation of this vast estate are commensurate with the princely manner in which Senator Stanford conducts all enterprises which he controls. The construction of the system was begun in 1882, and is not yet completed. The source of supply is Deer creek, which was tapped two and a half miles northeast of Vina, where two massive floodgates were constructed—one of wood and the other of granite laid in cement. The great central ditch has a grade of four feet to the mile and a capacity of 80,000 gallons per

minute, or 7,300 miner's inches. Two miles from its head a fifteen-
foot branch ditch begins and runs past the vineyard, supplying the
northern portion with water. This branch is sub-divided into ten
smaller ditches, nine of which run through the vineyard and are con-
trolled by a system of floodgates, which give uniform irrigation to
every foot of the vineyard.

A COMPREHENSIVE IRRIGATION SCHEME.

The tenth prong passes on through the vineyard a distance of two
miles, where it is subdivided into twenty smaller ditches for the irrigation of a five-hundred-acre field of alfalfa, each ditch, even at this
distance of five miles from Deer creek, being nine feet wide and running full in the dryest season. After supplying the northern fork,
the main ditch runs for a mile into a twenty-foot bottom, with a slope
of one and one-half to one, and then along the line of the railroad for
over four miles with a thirty-foot bottom and with a grade of two feet
to the mile. From this, nineteen six-foot ditches branch out and are
carried through the new portions of the vineyard. Opposite the head
of the main ditch, a third ditch, with a twelve-foot bottom, runs for
two miles to a six-hundred-acre alfalfa field, which it intersects with a
series of cross ditches, making altogether a system of fifty-five miles
of ditches, capable of irrigating 12,000 acres. The water rights of the
Vina ranch are secure for all time, thanks to the foresight of its
owner, who secured the land along Deer creek, which commands
them, thus adding, with the irrigating system, fully a half million
dollars to the value of the estate.

The land which is devoted to the raising of alfalfa is the richest
bottom land on the ranch, and immensely productive. The first hay
crop is cut in May, after which the water is turned on, and with the
stimulus of the hot sun, another larger crop is ready for the mowers
in six weeks. In this way four crops are taken from the same land,
averaging six tons of hay to the acre per season, of a sweet and most
nutritious quality, which is baled and stored for future use or market.
After the last crop the cattle are turned upon the land, where they
revel in the juiciest of food during the winter.

The wheat land, a light alluvial, lies along the river, and is very
productive.

A MAGNIFICENT DOMAIN.

It is separated into natural park-like divisions, formed by belts of
timber running back from the stream to the hill land.   These alter-

nate stretches of thousands of acres of field and forest, with great oaks dotting the golden stubble, give this portion of the ranch the appearance of a vast, magnificent, well-kept park. The other portions of the estate come under the head of "plain and foot-hills grazing land." Thus far they have been put to no other use than for pasture; but it was the intention of Senator Stanford to test the hill land by setting out vineyards, as it is his belief that much of it is valuable for grape-growing. The live-stock on the estate is very valuable, and consists of 20,000 sheep, 86 mules, 270 horses, 800 hogs, 70 thorough-bred cows, 30 thorough-bred calves and bulls, and 200 common cattle. The products of the ranch at the present time are, of course, small compared with its size, but this will be understood when it is considered that the property has just been taken in hand, and that a small portion, only, of the vineyard is in bearing. This year it produced 1,000 tons of grapes, from which 100,000 gallons of wine were made; 900 tons of alfalfa, 400 sacks of barley, 15,000 sacks of wheat, 500 tons of oaten hay and a large amount of vegetables.

There is a comfortable mansion on the place, with good barns, granaries and dwellings for the employees, outhouses, etc. A new winery was built last spring, the first floor of which contains two hundred casks, holding 1,500 gallons each, seventy of which are now full. On the second floor are two steam grape crushers, with a capacity of twenty tons an hour each. Back of the winery is the engine room and distillery, which are complete in every department. Although this winery is a large one, its capacity will have to be increased many times when the 3,000 and odd acres of vineyard come into full bearing.

Taken altogether, with its fine soil, excellent location, unsurpassed irrigation facilities and good climate, the Vina ranch cannot but prove immensely productive when subdivided into small farms and thoroughly and carefully cultivated.

THE GRIDLEY RANCH.

The gridley ranch, the third of Senator Stanford's magnificent gifts, is one of California's great wheat farms. It is situated in Butte county, and comprises from 19,000 to 21,000 acres of as rich wheat land as can be found in the wheat producing sections of the State. Some idea may be gained of its productive qualities when it is stated that an average yield of forty-five bushels per acre is not unusual. At the present time this vast tract of land, all suitable for cultivation, is used only for the raising of grain, and whether it can be profitably utilized for other purposes, when cut up into small farms, remains to be seen. It is a princely gift, worthy of the donator, and stands assessed this year at $1,000,000.

BIOGRAPHICAL SKETCH OF HON. LELAND STANFORD.

The future historian of the Pacific Coast will assign to Leland Stanford a prominent place in the stirring events accompanying the wonderful growth and development of California. As the master spirit of that great work, the Central Pacific Railroad, had he done nothing further to entitle him to the gratitude of the people, his name would have gone down to posterity as a public benefactor; but when we consider what he has done, and proposes to do, in the cause of education, the character of the man assumes a grandeur which challenges universal admiration.

Leland Stanford was born in Albany county, New York, on the ninth day of March, 1824. The alternation of work upon the home-stead farm with study at a neighboring school, after the manner of the sons of intelligent and thrifty farmers in those days, contributed to give him that well-balanced mind, keen perception and perfect equipose of faculties for which he has ever been distinguished. Endowed by nature with a powerful physical organization, he was, in youth, somewhat impatient of purely scholastic methods, which imposed too much indoor constraint upon a mind linked to a body full of vigorous life, which demanded a large degree of freedom and exercise in the open air. But this very impatience of confinement threw wide open to him the book of nature, laid the foundation for an enthusiastic love of the natural sciences, and made him a keen and discriminating observer of material things; a kind of education, well adapted to fit him for the great enterprises and the high and responsible trusts in which he has distinguished himself. At twenty years of age, with such education as he had gathered by this somewhat desultory method, he determined upon the study of the law, and entered the office of Messrs. Wheaton, Doolittle and Hadley, an eminent law firm in the city of Albany, in the year 1845. Having completed his studies, and been admitted to the bar, he resolved to seek in the West, a field for his future professional labors, and finally settled at Port

Washington, Wisconsin, in 1848. Two years afterward, he returned to Albany and was there married to a most estimable young lady, Miss Jane Lathrop, daughter of Dyer Lathrop, a merchant and one of the most respected citizens of Albany. His professional career in his Wisconsin home was of brief duration. While practicing law at Port Washington, a circumstance transpired which some will regard as providential, giving an entirely new direction to his thoughts and energies. A fire occurred which destroyed his law library and swept away nearly all his worldly possessions. The loss was severe, and to one possessing less self-reliance would have been disheartening. It served, however, its purpose, and the result was, a determination on his part to join his brothers, who had already emigrated to California. He reached this State on the twelfth day of July, 1852, and found his brothers engaged in mining and trade. Without any practical knowledge of either of these occupations, Mr. Stanford determined for the time to abandon the practice of the law and engage in business with his brothers. After prospecting at various points he finally settled at Michigan Bluff, in the famous mining county of Placer, where he remained nearly four years conducting in a very successful manner the business in which he was engaged, and making a host of friends among the hardy pioneers and miners who were his principal patrons. In 1856, he removed to Sacramento, and as a partner became actively engaged in the mercantile house established by his brothers, whose business had grown to large proportions, they being extensively engaged in importing, and having branch houses scattered through the State. The magnitude of the firm's transactions, the multifarious knowledge demanded and the natural aptitude of Mr. Stanford's mind for the administration of affairs of importance, all combined to develop and enlarge those extraordinary powers of observation and generalization which were subsequently displayed in the execution of the gigantic railway projects, which he undertook and carried through with such energy and success. At the breaking out of the civil war, Mr. Stanford was a most pronounced friend of the Union. He was chosen a delegate to the Chicago Convention in 1860, and voted for Abraham Lincoln, as the Republican candidate for the Presidency. The acquaintance which he there made with Mr. Lincoln, ripened into intimacy and confidence, and Mr. Stanford spent many weeks at Washington after the inauguration and became the trusted adviser of the President and his Cabinet, in regard to the appointments for the Pacific Coast. It is not one of the least of Mr. Stanford's honors, that in the perilous crisis of affairs which occurred in 1860, when California was in danger of following the bad example of the South, Mr. Lincoln and Mr. Seward, regarded him as the ablest and most reliable friend of the Government in this State and deferred to his opinion accordingly. In 1861, Mr. Stanford, contrary to his wishes, was nominated by the Republican party for Governor of California, and, while he sought no political preferment, he deemed it his duty, in the disturbed state of affairs to sacrifice his own wishes to the welfare of the State and Nation. He accordingly entered actively into the canvass and was elected by a plurality of twenty-three thousand votes. The period was one of unexampled difficulty of administration, but Governor Stanford was equal to all the demands made upon him, and however great his achievements, he never seemed to have exhausted his resources or to have reached his full possibilities. His messages, and indeed all his State papers, were characterized by sound common sense and a comprehensive grasp of State and National affairs, remarkable in one who had never before held office under either the State or National government. At the close of his term he had the satisfaction of leaving the chair of State, feeling that no State of the Union was more thoroughly loyal than California.

Governor Stanford was urged to accept a renomination, but being then thoroughly engrossed in the construction of the great transcontinental railway and feeling that the crisis in the history of the State which had compelled his acceptance in the first instance was now passed, he declined the proffered honor. At the last regular session of our State Legislature, he was elected United States Senator, which high position he has since filled with marked ability and to the entire satisfaction of the people. His establishment and endowment of the great University which bears the name of his lamented son, will go down to history as an act unparalleled in the annals of public benefactions, and his memory will ever be cherished in the hearts of a grateful people.

EPILOGUE

In all these circumstances I'll instruct you:
Go with me to clothe you as becomes you. — The Taming of the Shrew, iv.2

While patriarchs do not have to possess the originality of founders, they at least can be expected to lend a certain venerability to an institution that otherwise would be lacking. There can be no complaints on that score about the initial four and twenty guardians.

Senator Stanford's pick of men is worthy of more thought than it has been given. It would be difficult to argue that the founding trustees have received the attention that they deserve. A book-length prosopographical study of them would reveal a good deal about late nineteenth-century California, and about early Stanford University. Until then, speculation about their collective mentality remains speculation. One at least can safely claim that they were formidable, and that their sartorial style and hair styles suggest an ability to assume more active roles if called upon.

That of course is not to assert that the look of character and real success of character are the same. Flügel, a firm believer in the idea that clothes can be "symbolic of duty or moral control", severely warns about the great distortions of reality that a carefully cultivated appearance can achieve. There is, he remarks, "no essential connection between, say, a black coat and tight, stiff collar and the due sense of responsibility and duty for which these garments stand." To what extent the dour clothes, beards and muttonchops concealed provocative differences and picaresque disparities remains an intriguing challenge for Stanford historians.

✻ ✻ ✻

SELECTED BIBLIOGRAPHY

Joyce Asser. *Historic Hairdressing*. Sir Isaac Pitman and Sons, London, 1966.

Iris Brooke. *A History of English Costume*. Third Edition. Methuen & Co., London, 1968.

Penelope Byrde. *The Male Image*. B.T.Batsford, London, 1979.

Doriece Colle. *Collars, Stocks and Cravats: A History and Costume Dating Guide to Civilian Men's Neckpieces, 1655-1900*. British Edition. White Lion, London, 1974.

Richard Corson. *Fashions in Hair*. Revised. Peter Owen, London 1977.

Orrin Leslie Elliott. *Stanford University: The First Twenty-Five Years*. Stanford University Press, 1937.

J.C.Flügel. *The Psychology of Clothes*, The International Psycho-Analytical Library No.18. Hogarth Press, London, 1930.

Helen Lefkowitz Horowitz. *Campus Life: Undergraduate Cultures From the End of the Eighteenth Century to the Present*. Alfred A. Knopf, New York, 1987.

Orrin E. Klapp. *Symbolic Leaders*. Aldine, Chicago, 1964.

Claude Lévi-Strauss. *Totemism*, translated by Rodney Needham. Beacon Press, Boston, 1963.

Sarah Levitt. *Victorians Unbuttoned: Registered Designs for Clothing, their Makers and Wearers, 1839-1900*. George Allen & Unwin, London, 1986.

Reginald Reynolds. *Beards: Their Social Standing, Religious Involvements, Decorative Possibilities and Value in Offence and Defence Through the Ages*. Harcourt Brace Jovanovich, New York, 1976 (1949).

Frank H.T.Rhodes and Don E. Fehrenbacher. *Words Worth a Second Thought*. Stanford Centennial Committee, 1986.

Marion Sichel. *The Victorians*, Costume Reference 6. Plays, Boston, 1978.

Stanford Historical Society. *Sandstone and Tile*. Irregular.

Norman E. Tutorow. *The Early Years of Leland Stanford*. DeWitt Historical Society of Tompkins County, Ithaca (New York), 1969.

Norman E. Tutorow. *Leland Stanford: Man of Many Careers*. Pacific Coast Publishers, Menlo Park (California), 1971.

❋